WHERE CODE MEETS LIFE LESSONS

YASH HACKZ

To everyone who dared to ask **"why?"** when others simply accepted **"how."**
To the curious minds who never stopped questioning, learning, and evolving, even when the path seemed unclear.
This book is a reflection of the journey I've traveled—from the challenges of hacking the system to the growth of hacking my own limitations.

To my mentors and peers, whose guidance and support have been my compass in the ever-changing world of cybersecurity. To the family and friends who believed in me, even when the hours were long and the journey uncertain.

And, most importantly, to my younger self—who found inspiration in the unknown and courage in the face of adversity.
This book is as much yours as it is mine

Contents

FOREWORD

In a world increasingly shaped by technology, the line between what's ethical and what's not is often blurred. The internet, with its vast array of possibilities, can be both a tool for innovation and a playground for exploitation. This is where ethical hackers come in—not just to break into systems, but to build stronger ones, to push the boundaries of security, and to ensure that the digital world remains a safer place for all.

This book is more than just a collection of tips and tricks; it's a reflection of a personal journey, one that's been shaped by the pursuit of knowledge, the thrill of problem-solving, and the challenges of navigating an ever-evolving digital landscape. The art of ethical hacking is not only about mastering the technical skills—it's about understanding the responsibility that comes with it, the ethical considerations, and the unyielding curiosity that drives the hacker's mindset.

As you read through these pages, you'll find practical advice for anyone looking to break into the world of cybersecurity—from the foundational principles to the advanced techniques that define a skilled ethical hacker. But you'll also discover the story of a person who, like many others, began with nothing but curiosity and the desire to understand how things work beneath the surface. Along the way, there were moments of failure, of doubt, and of triumph. It's a journey that's not just about hacking technology—but also about hacking life.

The lessons shared here are not only technical in nature but are deeply personal. They reflect the highs and lows, the setbacks and breakthroughs that come with pursuing a passion and carving your own path. It's a story of growth, resilience, and the unwavering belief that knowledge—when used for good—can change the world.

Whether you're an aspiring ethical hacker, a seasoned cybersecurity professional, or someone simply interested in understanding the world of hacking from an ethical perspective,

PREFACE

When I first stumbled upon the world of ethical hacking, I was just a curious individual—an inquisitive mind eager to understand how things worked, particularly the systems that governed the digital world around me. Little did I know, that curiosity would grow into a passion that would shape not only my career but my very identity. This book is the culmination of years spent learning, experimenting, failing, and succeeding in the field of cybersecurity. It is a guide, a toolkit, and a memoir—all rolled into one. But more than that, it's a reflection of my own journey, the lessons I've learned along the way, and the personal struggles I've faced in balancing my passion for hacking with the ethical responsibilities that come with it.

Through this book, I want to share not only the tips and tricks I've accumulated over the years, but also the lessons learned from my personal experiences—both the successes and the failures. I'll take you through the technical side of ethical hacking: from understanding how vulnerabilities are exploited to mastering penetration testing techniques. But I'll also give you a glimpse into my life: the setbacks, the late nights, the self-doubt, and the triumphs. You'll read about the moments when everything clicked, and the moments when I hit a wall, only to learn something new and unexpected.

Thank you for joining me on this journey. I hope that, like me, you'll come to see ethical hacking not just as a profession, but as a lifelong pursuit—a path that is as much about personal growth as it is about protecting the digital world.

ACKNOWLEDGEMENTS

Writing this book has been an incredible journey—one that would not have been possible without the support, encouragement, and inspiration from so many people along the way. It is my honor to express my heartfelt gratitude to all those who have played a part in shaping both the content of this book and my personal journey in the world of ethical hacking. First and foremost, I want to thank my family for their unwavering belief in me. To my parents, whose constant encouragement allowed me to explore the unknown without fear of failure, thank you for giving me the courage to pursue my passions, no matter how unconventional they seemed. To my friends, who have been my sounding boards during late-night coding sessions and offered advice when I needed it most—you are my pillars of support. To my colleagues in the cybersecurity industry, thank you for fostering an environment of collaboration and growth. Your insights, constructive criticism, and shared experiences have made me a better hacker and a more responsible professional. This book reflects the knowledge and practices that have been passed down through our community, and I am proud to contribute my voice to that collective wisdom.

Finally, to my younger self—the one who first discovered hacking as a way to understand the world and find solutions to its problems—this book is a tribute to you. I've come a long way since then, and I can only hope that anyone reading this will feel encouraged to embark on their own journey, no matter how intimidating the road may seem.

Thank you all for being part of this journey. I hope you find as much inspiration and knowledge in these pages as I have in the process of writing them.

PROLOGUE

There was a time when I sat at my desk, staring at the screen, wondering how the world around me worked—how systems were built, how information flowed through networks, and how people could exploit vulnerabilities that I could hardly understand. Like many who start their journey into ethical hacking, I had no grand plan. I was simply driven by a deep curiosity, a desire to learn, and a determination to solve puzzles. This book is a reflection of my journey into that world. It's a blend of technical knowledge—ethical hacking tips and tricks that I've picked up along the way—and personal experiences, struggles, and breakthroughs that have shaped my path. Over the years, I've learned that ethical hacking isn't just about knowing how to break into a system; it's about understanding how to protect it, how to think like an attacker while acting with integrity, and how to apply your skills for the greater good. I've made mistakes. I've stumbled. And I've faced moments of doubt. But it's through those challenges that I grew—not only as a hacker, but as a person. I've learned the importance of persistence, resilience, and, perhaps most importantly, the power of ethical decision-making in a world where the lines between right and wrong can sometimes blur.

So, if you're ready to unlock the secrets of cybersecurity, embrace the challenges ahead, and learn the true art of ethical hacking, let's begin.

Yash Hackz is an Indian Ethical Hacker. And YouTuber who works with various organizations as a Cybersecurity Analyst. He conducted numerous seminars at various colleges, training students in the fields of cybersecurity and ethical hacking. He recently completed his 12th standard education at **AM World School Chandaushi**, and is now focused on furthering his studies. Yash writes to inspire hope in those seeking it. With over 17,000 followers on Instagram (@yash__hackz), his words resonate deeply with his readers. If you enjoy this book, please reach out to Yash at @yash__hackz on Instagram. He'd love to hear from you!

"WHERE CODE MEETS LIFE LESSONS"

Yash Hackz,

"This Book will make you feel too many things, all at once. just like life does sometimes....."

yash hackz

• xviii •

Introduction

In "Where Code Meets Life Lessons" I aim to explore the profound connections between the technical world of Ethical Hacking and Cybersecurity and the personal journey we navigate in our lives. This book serves as a guide to understanding how the principles of programming and cybersecurity can provide valuable insights into our daily experiences, fostering a deeper understanding of resilience, ethics, and adaptability. Through sharing my personal anecdotes—from the challenges of my early coding days to the lessons learned from significant cybersecurity incidents—I hope to offer readers a relatable perspective. Each chapter intertwines practical tips with life lessons, empowering you to approach both your professional pursuits and personal growth with a renewed mindset. As we embark on this journey together, I encourage you to reflect on your own experiences and apply the insights gained here to become not only a better coder or cybersecurity professional but also a more thoughtful and engaged individual in every facet of your life.....

I

Ethical Hacking- understanding the basics

Overview of Ethical Hacking :- Ethical hacking, often referred to as penetration testing or white-hat hacking, involves authorized individuals who simulate cyberattacks on systems to identify vulnerabilities and strengthen security measures. Unlike malicious hackers, ethical hackers operate within legal and ethical boundaries, working to protect organizations from cyber threats.

- **Purpose** :- The primary goal of ethical hacking is to enhance security by identifying and fixing vulnerabilities before they can be exploited by malicious actors. This proactive approach helps organizations safeguard sensitive data and maintain their integrity.

Types of Hackers:-
1. **White Hat Hackers (Ethical Hackers)**

1. Purpose: To improve security by finding and fixing vulnerabilities.
2. Activities: Conduct authorized penetration testing, security assessments, and audits
3. Characteristics: Operate within legal and ethical boundaries; often work for organizations or as consultants.

Black Hat Hackers :-

1. Purpose: To exploit vulnerabilities for malicious intent, such as stealing data, spreading malware, or causing damage.
2. Activities: Conduct illegal hacking activities, including data breaches and financial theft
3. Characteristics: Operate outside legal and ethical boundaries; driven by personal gain, ideology, or notoriety.

Gray Hat Hackers :-

1. Purpose: To find vulnerabilities without permission but typically without malicious intent.
2. Activities: May notify organizations of vulnerabilities or exploit them for personal gain (though not usually malicious).
3. Characteristics: Operate in a morally ambiguous area; can sometimes transition between white and black hat hacking

"THE IMPORTANCE OF CYBERSECURITY ?"

With increasing cyber threats, organizations must prioritize cybersecurity. Ethical hackers play a crucial role in strengthening defenses and protecting sensitive information.

II

How beginners can get into the Cybersecurity As an Ethical Hacker

Learn the Basics of Cybersecurity :-

1. **Familiarize Yourself with Key Concepts**: Learn about networks, systems, and common threats like malware, phishing, and social engineering.
2. **Online Resources**: Websites like Cybrary, Coursera, or Udemy offer introductory courses on cybersecurity fundamentals

Learn Programming Languages -

1. **Start with Basics**: Focus on languages commonly used in security, such as Python, JavaScript, or Bash scripting
2. **Understand Scripting**: Scripting is essential for automation and understanding how exploits work.

<u>Get Hands-On Experience</u> :-

1. **Set Up a Home Lab**: Use virtual machines to create a safe environment for testing and learning.
2. **Practice with Tools**: Familiarize yourself with tools like Wireshark, Metasploit, and Nmap.

- **Get Familiar with Networking Tools :-**

Learn to use common networking and security tools, such as:

1. **Wireshark**: A network packet analyzer that helps you capture and analyze network traffic.
2. **Nmap**: A network scanner used to discover hosts and services on a computer network.
3. **Netcat**: A tool for network communication, used for creating reverse shells.
4. **Burp Suite**: A suite of tools for web application security testing.

Learn Ethical Hacking Techniques

- Study the core areas of ethical hacking and penetration testing, including:

1. **Reconnaissance (Information Gathering)**: Techniques like footprinting and scanning to gather information about your target system.
2. **Vulnerability Analysis**: Tools like Nessus or OpenVAS are used to scan systems for vulnerabilities.
3. **Exploitation**: Using vulnerabilities to access a system. This may involve exploiting bugs in software, misconfigurations, weak passwords, etc
4. **Post-Exploitation**: Techniques for maintaining access to a system, escalating privileges, and gathering sensitive data.

5. **Social Engineering**: Techniques like phishing, baiting, and pretexting to manipulate people into giving access to systems or data.

Certifications to Pursue :---------

- Certifications are a good way to validate your skills and gain credibility. Here are some popular cybersecurity certifications for beginners:

1. **CompTIA Security+**: A good entry-level certification covering the basics of cybersecurity.
2. **Certified Ethical Hacker (CEH)**: A certification specifically designed for ethical hackers that covers various hacking techniques and countermeasures.
3. **Offensive Security Certified Professional (OSCP)**: A more advanced certification that focuses on hands-on penetration testing.

Join the Cybersecurity Community

- Engage with the cybersecurity community to stay updated and learn from others. Some popular communities include:
- **Reddit**: Subreddits like r/netsec, r/AskNetsec, or r/ethicalhacking.
- **Discord/Slack Channels**: Many groups are dedicated to ethical hacking and cybersecurity.
- **Conferences**: Attend events like DEF CON, Black Hat, or OWASP conferences to meet professionals and expand your knowledge.

Stay Updated and Practice

- ***As we all know practice makes a man perfect.***

III

Hacking Techniques

We will start from basic......

- **Phishing** :- Phishing is a type of online scam used by hackers, where someone tries to trick you into giving away personal information, like your passwords, credit card numbers, or social security number.

Here's how it works -

1. **Fake messages**: You get an email, text, or message that looks like it's from a company or person you trust, like your bank or an online store.
2. **Urgency:** The message often says something urgent, like "Your account is locked!" or "You need to confirm your identity right now!"
3. **Fake links or attachments**: The message asks you to click on a link or open an attachment, which may look real but actually takes you to a fake website or downloads a harmful file.
4. **The goal**: Once you enter your personal info (like your username, password, or credit card number), the scammer steals it and can use it for fraud or identity theft.

How To make Our Own Phishing Link ?

- There are lots of tools are available online by which you can use to make your own phishing link . One of my favourite Tool is Zphisher that you can use to make your own phishing link You can install that tool in your linux with the help of github
  here's the link - https://github.com/htr-tech/zphisher

How Zphisher Works ?

1. **Pre-configured Templates:** ZPhisher provides pre-built templates for popular websites and services, such as Facebook, Instagram, Google, Twitter, etc. These templates mimic the real login pages of these services.
2. **Phishing Attack**: Once the attacker sets up the fake login page, they can share a link to it. When a victim enters their login credentials on the fake page, the attacker collects that information.
3. **Credential Theft:** The attacker can then use the stolen credentials to access the victim's accounts, steal sensitive data, or commit identity theft.

   "**Warning:** *This method should be used for legal purposes only. Any illegal use of this tool, including phishing or unauthorized data collection, is punishable by law and can result in severe legal consequences. Always ensure you have proper consent and authorization before conducting any security tests.*"

Ddos Attack :- A DDoS attack stands for Distributed Denial of Service. It's a type of cyberattack where a group of computers or devices is used to overwhelm a website or online service with more traffic than it can handle, causing it to slow down or even crash.

Simple Example:

- Imagine a restaurant that can only serve 100 people at a time. Normally, the restaurant gets 100 customers, and everyone gets their food in a reasonable amount of time. But now, imagine that 1,000 people show up all at once and start crowding the entrance, blocking the door, and making it impossible for the regular customers to get in. The restaurant becomes overwhelmed and can't serve anyone.

   In the same way, a DDoS attack sends too much data to a website, flooding the server, which then can't handle all the requests, making it crash or become very slow.

Why Do People Do It?

1. **Disrupting business**: Some attackers might use DDoS attacks to take down a business website or service temporarily, hurting the company.
2. **Protesting:** Some attacks are politically motivated, where a group targets a company or government to make a statement.
3. **Extortion**: Attackers might launch a DDoS attack and demand money to stop it.

How To Perform ddos attack ?

- Also There are lots of tools available online for performing Ddos Attack. **Goldeneye** is also an good tool for performing Ddos Attack. You can visit github url for more information.

Call Spoofing :- Call spoofing is when someone changes the phone number that appears on your caller ID. Instead of showing their real number, they make it look like the call is coming from a different number, often one that looks familiar or trustworthy.

- **For example**, a spammer might make their call appear as if it's coming from your bank or a local business, even though it's not. This is done using special software or services, and the goal is usually to trick you into answering the call or providing personal information.

One more example, suppose you can call your friend with his father phone number. Without even touching anyone's phone. Yes this is possible with call spoofing. Now you can understand how much dangerous it is.....

It's important to be cautious when receiving unexpected calls, especially if the number seems suspicious or you weren't expecting a call from that place

- **How To Perform Call Spoofing ?**

This is done using special Software or services, For trial you can use Indy call apk that is available for android using that application you can perform call spoofing. But free version provides you limited use only. For unlimited times use, simply you can clear the apk data and use it multiple times

> "*Warning: This method should be used for legal purposes only. Any illegal use of this tool, is punishable by law and can result in severe legal consequences. Always ensure you have proper consent and authorization before conducting any security tests.*"

Keylogger :- A keylogger is a type of computer program or device that secretly records everything you type on your keyboard.

- Imagine you're typing on your computer, and someone is secretly watching every word you type without you knowing. A keylogger does just that—it keeps track of all the keys you press, like passwords, messages, or anything else you type.

-

- **Keyloggers** are often used by hackers to steal private information, like your passwords or credit card numbers, without you realizing it. They can be installed on your computer without your knowledge, either by opening a harmful link or downloading a bad file.

To stay safe, it's important to have good security software and be cautious about what you click on or download.

- **How To Make own Keylogger ?**
- If you want to make your own keylogger. You can create it by using python language or other resources.

- **Brute Force Attack** :- A **brute force attack** is a way of trying to break into something, like an account or a computer system, by guessing the password over and over until the correct one is found. Imagine you have a locked door and you're trying every possible key, one by one, until the door opens.
-

- **How To Perform Brute Force Attack ?**
- There are lots of tools available for brute force attack I'd suggest you **Hydra** is a good tool for performing brute force attack. You can download and use it in your Kali Linux.

Email Spoofing :- Email spoofing is just like call spoofing. Email spoofing is when someone sends an email that looks like it came from a trusted person or company, but it's actually from someone else.

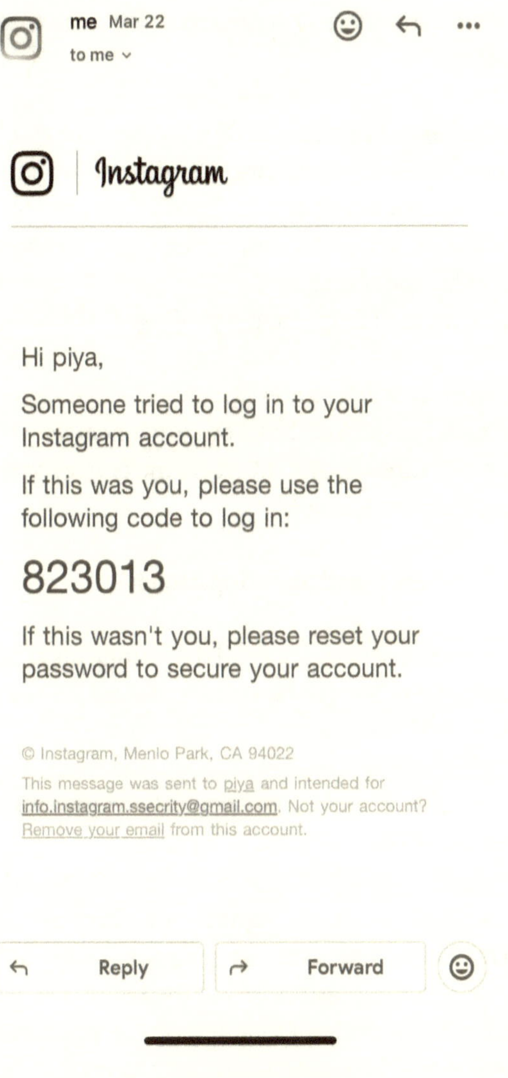

Email Spoofing

imagine you get an email that looks like it's from your instagram, saying someone tried to log in to yout instagram account and asking you to click a link to reset your password But in reality, the email wasn't sent by instagra; it was sent by a bad person (a hacker) who made the email look like it came from them. This trick is called **"email spoofing."**

- The goal of email spoofing is often to deceive you into clicking on harmful links or giving away sensitive information, like your password or credit card details. Spoofing is possible because the "From" field in an email can be changed easily, so it doesn't always reflect the real sender.
- To protect yourself from email spoofing:

1. Be careful of unsolicited emails.
2. Don't click on suspicious links or attachments.
3. Verify emails directly by contacting the person or company that supposedly sent the email.

How To Perform Email Spoofing Attack ?

- There are lots of videos are available online on email spoofing. I have also created a video on email spoofing. You can do check it out

-

- Here's the link of tutorial :- https://www.instagram.com/reel/CODuvMTPE6R/?igsh=Ym1vc2ZjNzk0aGY3

What is Beef :- Beef stands for **Browser Exploitation Framework**. It's a tool used by security professionals, ethical hackers, or penetration testers to test the security of web browsers. But, just to be clear, it's also a tool that can be misused by hackers if they're doing illegal activities, so it's very important to understand how it's used responsibly.

- **What does BeEF do?**
- BeEF is used to find weaknesses in a web browser. A web browser is the program you use to browse websites, like Chrome, Firefox,

or Safari. BeEF allows someone (usually a security expert) to test the browser's security by creating fake attacks on the browser to see if it has any vulnerabilities that could be exploited.

How To Hack Web Browsers using Beef Tool ?

- You Can Download Beef Tool in Kali Linux. For more information, you can visit
- Github url - https://github.com/beefproject/beef

What is CSRF :- **CSRF** stands for **Cross-Site Request Forgery**. It's a type of attack that tricks a user into doing something they didn't intend to do on a website, where they're already logged in.

Imagine This Scenario:

- You are logged into a banking website, and you have your account open. Now, let's say you visit another website (maybe a random blog or a malicious website). While you're on that site, an attacker has hidden a special request that looks like it's coming from you.
- Because you're already logged into your bank account, the bank doesn't know that this request isn't really from you. It just assumes it's you asking for something, like transferring money to someone else's account.

How Does It Work?

1. You're logged in to a site (like your bank).
2. You visit another website that has hidden code (like a malicious image or link) that automatically sends a request to your bank.
3. Your bank sees the request and thinks it's legitimate because it's coming from your browser where you're logged in.
4. The attacker gets what they want, maybe stealing your money or changing account details, without you knowing.

- **It seems dangerous Right ?**
- **Why is this a Problem?**
- The problem is that the attacker never needed your password or any login details. They only needed to trick you into making an action while you were logged into another website. It exploits the trust that websites have in their users' browsers.

How to Protect Against CSRF?

- To protect against CSRF, websites can use tokens. These tokens are like secret keys that are only known by the website and the user Whenever the website asks for a sensitive action (like transferring money), it also asks for the token. If the token is missing or doesn't match, the action is blocked. This makes it much harder for attackers to forge the request

in short, CSRF is like,

- someone tricking you into unknowingly clicking a button or link that does something bad on a website you're already logged into. It's dangerous because it doesn't need your password—just your session on the site!

CSRF

What is Camphish :- Camphish is made up of two words "Cam" & "phish" So, Camphish is a Kali Linux Tool its a mobile front camera hacking tool.

· **How Does it Works ?**

1. Hacker creates a malicious link and trick you to send that link. Whenever you click on that link it says allow permission if mistakely you allowed it. Then your phone front camera will be hacked hacker can veiw you untill the tab is open in your browser.

Which Type of Links Hackers can create ?

· They can create links for camphish like wishing you a very happy diwali , like you won an award to trick you to click on the malacious link.

What is RAT :- RAT stands for **Remote Access Trojan**. It's a type of malicious software (malware) that allows a hacker to secretly control your computer or device from a distance, without your knowledge. It hides on your device and lets an attacker secretly watch what you're doing, steal your files, or even control your keyboard and mouse as if they were sitting right in front of your screen.

- **How Does a RAT Work?**

Infection: A RAT usually gets onto your computer through things like:

1. Infected email attachments or malicious links.
2. Downloading shady software from untrusted websites.
3. Exploiting security holes in outdated software.

Hidden Operation: Once the RAT is installed, it runs in the background without you knowing. It might even hide itself by pretending to be a regular program or file on your computer.

1. Remote Control: The attacker, who is far away, can now access your computer. They can:

- View your screen.
- Capture your keystrokes (see what you type).
- Control your mouse (move it around).
- Steal files from your computer, such as photos, documents, or passwords.
- Turn on your camera or microphone without you knowing. !

Why is RAT Dangerous?

1. Complete Control: The attacker can control your computer as if they were sitting right in front of it.

2. Privacy Violations: They can spy on your personal information, such as passwords, bank details, and private conversations.
3. Data Theft: Sensitive files, documents, photos, and even emails can be stolen.
4. Use Your Device for Bad Things: Hackers can also use your computer to attack other systems, send spam, or launch other malicious actions.

Imagine,

- You get an email from someone you don't know with an attachment that seems harmless, like a picture or a document. You open the file, and without realizing it, you've downloaded a RAT onto your computer. The hacker can now see what's happening on your screen, steal yourfiles, or even use your *webcam to watch you*.

How to Protect Yourself from RATs?

1. Avoid Suspicious Emails: Don't open attachments or click on links from people you don't trust, especially if they seem strange or unexpected.
2. Use Antivirus Software: A good antivirus program can help detect and remove RATs.
3. Keep Your Software Updated: Make sure your operating system and apps are always up to date to protect against security holes.
4. Be Careful with Downloads: Only download software from trusted, official websites.
5. Use a Firewall: A firewall can help block unwanted connections and monitor network traffic for suspicious activity.

In Simple Terms:

- **A RAT (Remote Access Trojan)** is like a secret hacker that sneaks into your computer, watches what you do, and sometimes even takes control of your computer without you knowing. It's dangerous because it can steal your personal information and cause a lot of harm. Always stay cautious about where you click and what you download to protect yourself from RATs!

"Wait.. Wait.. Wait do you know about binding ?"

Lemme tell you,

- Binding is a method, where a hacker can bind his rat with any other application. Like he can bind rat with instagram , whatsapp or any other application so that you can download the application easily. Or he can gain your device access.

Some Famous RATS are :-

- ***AndroRAT , Spynote , Flexispy , XploitSpy***

What is Metasploit :- Metasploit is a tool used by security experts (called ethical hackers or penetration testers) to test how vulnerable a computer or network is to hacking. It's like a "virtual hacker" that helps you check if there are weak spots in a system, before a real hacker can exploit them.

- Think of it like this: If you were building a castle, you would want to know where the weak spots in the walls are so enemies can't break in.
- Metasploit helps find those weak spots (vulnerabilities) in a system, and even shows how an attacker might break in through them.

"Metasploit is available in Kali Linux"

Now lets Learn about Payload :- Imagine you're a hacker (or an ethical hacker) trying to get into a locked system, like a computer or a network. You've found a way to open the door — that's the exploit (like finding a weakness in the system). But once the door is open, you need something to do inside the system. This is where the payload comes in. It's the "thing" that gets delivered into the system once the exploit has successfully worked, and it tells the system what to do after it's been broken into.

- **Think of it like this**:
- Exploit = The key that unlocks the door.
- Payload = The action you take after you're inside, like walking through the door and setting up shop

example of a Payload:

- Let's say you used a vulnerability in a system (like a weakness in software) to get in. Once you're inside, the payloadmight do things like:

1. Open a remote shell that lets you control the system (kind of like taking over the computer from afar).
2. Grab passwords or steal sensitive information.
3. Make the system open up a backdoor for future attacks.

Types of Payloads:

1. Meterpreter – This is a popular payload in Metasploit (a hacking tool). It gives the attacker full control over the system once it's delivered.
2. Reverse Shell – This type of payload sends a signal back to the hacker's machine, so they can control the system.
3. Bind Shell – Instead of the attacker connecting back, this payload opens a port on the victim's system, allowing the attacker to connect directly.

How To Create a Payload using Metasploit ?

- To create a Payload using metasploit there are lots of videos are available on Youtube like how to create a payload using metasploit. For more information you can visit the web
  Here's the link :-
  http://surl.li/plptjk
- If you have confusion by setting LHOST its your local ip. You can get it by executing the command ifconfig. For more information you can checkout any video tutorial. And LPORT you have to select default that is 4444.

How Hacker Can Change their ip address multiple times in just 1 second ?

1. We required a tool **kalitorify** to change ip address multiple times in just 2 seconds. You can install **kalitorify** in your kali linux For more information you can visit github url

- Here's the link :- https://github.com/brainfucksec/kalitorify

1. Video Tutorial :- http://surl.li/xpggms

Commands you can use for installing kalitorify :-

- git clone https://github.com/brainfucksec/kalitorify
- ls
- cd kalitorify
- sudo make install kalitorify
- -tor

Now, let's learn about :-

- **Information gathering** :- Imagine you want to learn about a person, a company, or a place. To do this, you might ask questions, read articles, check social media, or look up data in different sources. All these actions are ways of gathering information.

Why is Information Gathering Important?

- In cybersecurity, information gathering helps professionals understand how to protect systems or find weaknesses. Also it is usefull for social engineering.

For Example :- if i want to gather someone instagram information, there is a tool available on github **OSINTGRAM**. It helps to gather information about victim like his followings email, phone numbers what time he posted like such information.

- So, information gathering plays an important role in cybersecuity

Evil twin Attack :- An Evil Twin Attack is a type of cyber attack where an attacker sets up a fake Wi-Fi hotspot that looks like a legitimate one. The goal is to trick people into connecting to it, allowing the attacker to spy on their internet activity, steal sensitive information, or even infect their devices with malware.

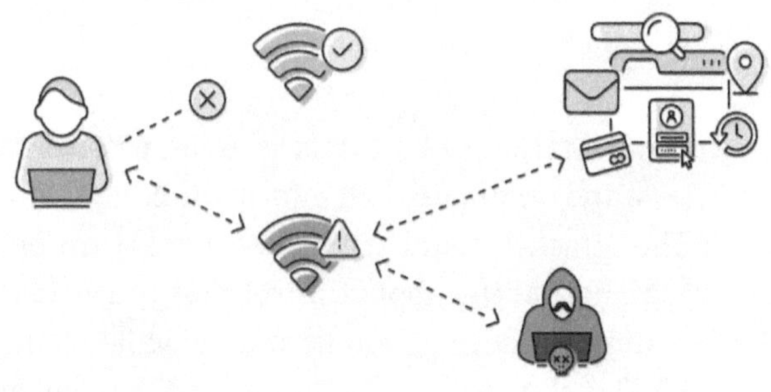

Evil twin Attack

How Does an Evil Twin Attack Work?

1. Fake Wi-Fi Network: The attacker creates a Wi-Fi network with a name (SSID) that is similar or identical to a legitimate Wi-Fi network that people trust. For example, the attacker might name their fake network

   "CoffeeShop_WiFi" while a real nearby network also has that name.
2. Deception: When you look for Wi-Fi networks on your phone or laptop, you'll see the attacker's fake Wi-Fi network listed, and it might even have a stronger signal than the real one. If you connect to it, you might think it's the official one.
3. Man-in-the-Middle: Once you connect to the fake network, the attacker can intercept all your internet traffic. This is called a Man-in-the-Middle attack because the attacker sits "in the middle" of your connection, observing everything you send or receive
4. Data Theft: If you're doing things like logging into websites, entering passwords, or using online banking, the attacker can capture that sensitive information. They might also be able to redirect you to fake websites that look real, tricking you into entering even more personal data.

   "It Seems dangerous right now? It is"

Why Is It Dangerous?

1. Data Theft: The attacker can steal usernames, passwords, credit card numbers, and other personal information.
2. Malware: The attacker could try to inject malware onto your device if you're not careful about the websites you visit.
3. Privacy Violations: Anything you do online while connected to the fake Wi-Fi network can be monitored by the attacker, including emails, messages, or browsing history.

How to Protect Yourself:

1. Be Careful When Connecting: Avoid connecting to public Wi-Fi networks that you don't trust. Look for networks with names you recognize, and be cautious if a network name looks too similar to a legitimate one.

For More information or want to learn more how evil twin attack works :-

- You can checkout this video :-
- http://surl.li/iirxcf

What is PasteJacking :-*Pastejacking* is a type of cyber attack where an attacker takes advantage of the "copy and paste" function on your device. It works by secretly replacing the text that you copy with something malicious when you try to paste it somewhere, like in a website form, email, or chat message.

- **How Does Pastejacking Work?**

1. Copying Text: Normally, when you copy text, like a web address or a password, you expect that when you paste it elsewhere (like into a website login form), it will appear exactly as you copied it.
2. Malicious Website or App: Pastejacking happens when you visit a malicious website or use an infected app. The website or app sneaks into your clipboard (the temporary storage area where your copied text is saved) and replaces the copied text with something else—usually something harmful, like a malicious link or a fake password.
3. Pasting the Wrong Text: When you try to paste the text into a form or message, you're actually pasting the malicious data (like a harmful link or an attacker's phone number) instead of what you originally copied.
4. Dangerous Consequences: This can trick you into clicking on a dangerous link, visiting a phishing site, or sending malicious links to others without realizing it. For example, if you copied a

legitimate URL for a website and then paste it into a form, you might end up pasting a malicious link that could steal your login details or install malware on your device.

Why Is Pastejacking Dangerous?

1. Phishing: The attacker might replace a copied URL with a fake, malicious one. You could then visit a fake login page, thinking it's the real one, and unknowingly give away your username and password.
2. Malware: If you paste something malicious, like a script or link, it could infect your device with malware.
3. Spreading Harm: If you paste malicious links into social media posts, emails, or messages, you could unknowingly spread malware to your friends or contacts.

In Simple Terms:

- Imagine you copy a website address like "example.com" to paste it into your browser, but when you paste it, you actually get a link like "evilwebsite.com" instead. If you click on the fake link, you might get tricked into giving away personal information or infect your device with a virus. Pastejacking is a sneaky attack that takes advantage of your trust in the copy-and-paste function. Always double-check what you're pasting, especially when dealing with sensitive information.

> *"Like you can understand how much dangerous pastejacking is if you're copying a bitcoin wallet address and if it replace with attacker wallet address."*

- **Warning: This method should be used for legal purposes only. Any illegal use of this tool, is punishable by law and can result in severe legal consequences. Always ensure you have proper consent and authorization before conducting any security**

tests.

What is Seeker :- Seeker is a tool used for social engineering attacks, specifically to gather information about a target using location tracking. It works by creating a fake website or link that tricks someone into clicking it. Once the person clicks on the link, the tool can capture details about their device, such as their IP address and location.

· **In Simple Terms:**

Seeker is like a trick that makes you click on a fake link, and when you do, the attacker can see where you are and what device you're using. It's a sneaky way of gathering information about you without your knowledge. Always be cautious before clicking on links, especially if you don't know who sent them!

· **Why Is Seeker Dangerous?**

1. Location Tracking: Seeker can give the attacker your real-time location, which could be used to track you or even cause harm.
2. Privacy Violation: It can invade your privacy by revealing personal information about your device and activities.
3. Social Engineering: If an attacker knows where you are, they might use that information to manipulate you, such as by convincing you to take certain actions based on your location or personal details.

How to Protect Yourself from Seeker?

1. Be Careful About Clicking Links: Never click on suspicious or unknown links, especially if they come from people you don't know or trust.
2. Check Link Addresses: Always hover over links before clicking them to make sure they lead to a trusted website.

3. Disable Location Services: On your mobile device or computer, you can disable location services to prevent apps from tracking your exact position.

For More information you can visit github url ....

- Here's the link :- https://github.com/thewhiteh4t/seeker

For installing Seeker Tool in your kali linux here are commands :-

- git clone https://github.com/thewhiteh4t/seeker.git
- cd seeker/
- chmod +x install.sh
- ./install.sh

What is DNS Spoofing :- DNS spoofing is like a "bad map" that sends you to the wrong destination. Instead of going to the website you intended, you end up at a fake site where attackers can steal your information or infect your device.

- **Simple Example:**

1. You type "facebook.com" into your browser.
2. Your computer asks the DNS where "facebook.com" is.
3. The attacker sends your computer the address of a fake Facebook page, even though it looks just like the real one.
4. You log in to that fake page, and the attacker steals your username and password.

The Result: You think you're visiting the real website, but you're actually on a fake version that the attacker controls. This can lead to:

1. Stealing your login details (like username and password).

2. Infecting your computer with malware.
3. Tricking you into giving away sensitive information

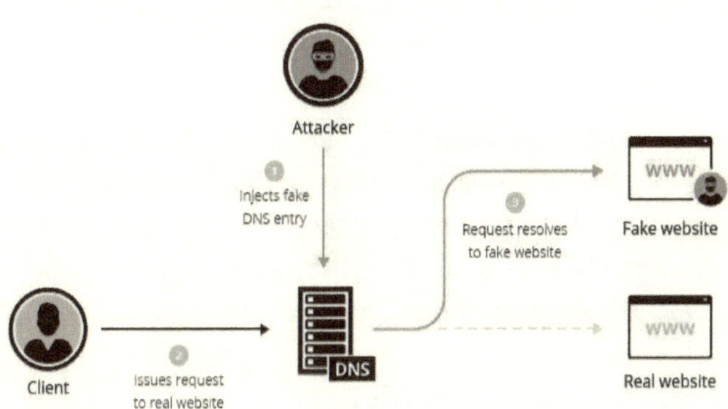

DNS Spoofing

"So, you can understand how much dangerous dns spoofing is"

What is Session hijacking :- Session hijacking is when a hacker steals your online "login session" and pretends to be you while you're still using the website. It's like someone sneaking into your account and doing things in your name without you knowing.

- **Example:**

1. You log in to your email, and everything seems fine.
2. A hacker secretly steals the "key" that proves you're logged in.
3. Now the hacker can read your emails, send messages, or change your settings, all while pretending to be you!

How Do Hackers Steal the Session?

- Hackers can steal your session token by using methods like:

1. Phishing (tricking you into giving them your login details).
2. Malware (installing harmful software on your device).
3. Man-in-the-middle attacks (eavesdropping on your connection to the website, often on public Wi-Fi)

Man-in-the-Middle Attack :- A *Man-in- the-Middle (MitM) Attack* is when a hacker secretly intercepts and possibly alters the communication between two parties—like you and a website, or you and a friend—without either party knowing. The hacker is like a "middleman" who can listen to or manipulate the conversation.

- **Here's how it works in simple terms:**
- Two Parties Communicate:

1. Normally, when you send a message or data online (like logging into a website or sending an email), your computer talks directly with the website or server.

"The Hacker's Role:"

In a Man-in-the-Middle Attack, the hacker secretly places themselves between you and the website (or between two people communicating). The hacker can read what you're sending, and in some cases, change what you're sending or receiving.

- **How the Hacker Intercepts:**

1. Imagine you're sending a message, but instead of going directly to your friend, it first goes through a hacker. The hacker reads the message, possibly changes it, and then sends it to your friend. Your friend never knows that the hacker was in the middle, so it seems like everything is normal.

- **Example:**

1. Wi-Fi: You connect to a free Wi-Fi network at a coffee shop. A hacker is also on that same Wi-Fi network. They can intercept the data between your phone and the websites you're visiting. If you're logging into your bank, the hacker can steal your login details.
2. Email: You send an email to a friend, but a hacker secretly intercepts the message, reads it, or even changes the content before your friend gets it.

Why It's Dangerous:

1. The hacker can steal sensitive information (like passwords, credit card numbers, or private messages).
2. They might also alter your communications, like changing the amount of money in a bank transaction or sending fake messages in your name.

In Simple Words:

- A Man-in-the-Middle attack is like someone secretly listening to and even changing a conversation between two people. The hacker is in the middle, without either party knowing, and they can steal information or cause problems.

How to Protect Yourself:

1. Use HTTPS: Look for "https://" in the website's address, which means the connection is encrypted and harder for hackers to intercept.
2. Avoid public Wi-Fi for sensitive activities (like online banking), or use a VPN to secure your connection
3. Enable two-factor authentication (2FA) to add extra security to your accounts.

yash hackz

BitB Attack :- in a Browser-in-the-Browser (BitB) attack, the hacker creates a fake login window that looks just like a real one from a trusted website (e.g., Facebook, Google, or your bank) But here's the twist: the fake login window appears inside your own web browser—it looks like it's part of the site you're visiting, but it's actually a clever imitation made by the attacker.

- **For Example :-**

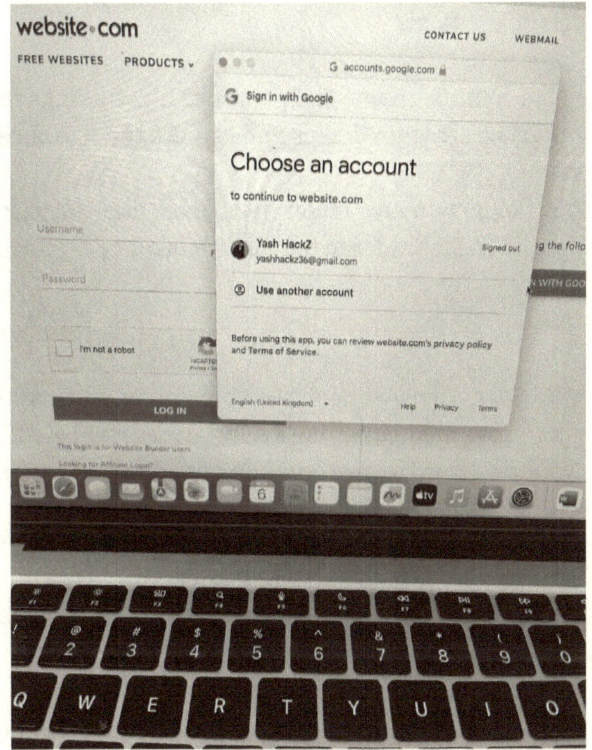

Bitb Attack

How It Looks:

1. You might see a pop-up or an "official- looking" login box that seems like it's from a real website (like your bank login). This pop-up will look very convincing, even showing the correct website URL.

2. The hacker's fake login window might even look exactly like the real website's login page, with the same design, fonts, and colors. You think you're entering your details into the official site, but you're really entering them into the fake login form.

What Happens Next?

1. If you type your username and password into this fake form, the attacker gets your login details and can use them to access your account.
2. The fake login window might even look like it's part of the website, making it harder to tell that it's fake.

Example:

1. You're browsing the web and see a pop- up window asking you to log in to your email account, saying something like "Please re-enter your password to continue." The window looks just like the official Google login page, but it's a fake.
2. You type in your username and password, thinking it's the real page, but the hacker now has your login information.

Why It's Dangerous:

1. Invisible Attack: It's hard to spot because the fake login window appears inside your own browser, and it looks just like the real thing.
2. Stolen Information: Once the hacker gets your login details, they can log into your accounts and steal information, make unauthorized transactions, or even lock you out of your own accounts.

In Simple Words:

- A Browser-in-the-Browser attack is when a hacker tricks you into entering your username and password into a fake login window that appears inside your own browser. The fake window looks like a real website login form, but it's actually a scam to steal your information.

How to Protect Yourself:

1. Check the URL: Make sure the website's address in the address bar is correct and that you're on a secure connection (look for https://).
2. Be Careful with Pop-ups: If a pop-up asks you to log in or enter sensitive info, be suspicious. It's better to type the website's address directly into the browser.
3. Enable Two-Factor Authentication (2FA): Even if a hacker steals your login details, they won't be able to access your account without the second verification step.

SQL injection :- SQL Injection is when a hacker tricks a website or app into running dangerous commands inside its database. This allows them to steal or change data, and sometimes even break the website or access sensitive information, all by entering special, harmful code into places like login forms or search boxes.

- **How does SQL Injection work?**

1. When you visit a website and fill out a form (like logging in or searching for something), the website uses SQL to talk to its database and find the information you asked for (like verifying your password or searching for a product).
2. In an SQL injection attack, the hacker enters malicious SQL code instead of regular input (like typing "OR 1=1" in a login form) to trick the website's database into doing something harmful, such as:

- Bypassing login: Getting into an account without the correct password.
- Stealing data: Extracting personal data like usernames, passwords, and emails from the database.
- Deleting or altering data: Changing information in the database or even deleting everything.

Example of SQL Injection:

1. Imagine a website with a login form where you enter your username and password.
2. A typical SQL query might look like this:

- SELECT * FROM users WHERE username =
     'user_input' AND password =
     'password_input';

1. This query checks if the username and password match what's stored in the database.
2. If the hacker enters this as their username:

- ' OR 1=1 --

The SQL query becomes:

- SELECT * FROM users WHERE username = " OR

1=1 -- AND password = ";

1. The OR 1=1 part always makes the condition true, so the database might think they've entered the right username and password.
2. The -- part tells the database to ignore the rest of the query, so the password check is skipped.
3. As a result, the hacker might be able to log in as an admin without knowing the correct password.

IV

Bug Bounty

What is bug bounty ?

- A **bug bounty** is a program that companies or organizations run to find and fix security vulnerabilities (or "bugs") in their software or website. Instead of trying to find the bugs themselves, they offer a reward, often called a "bounty," to anyone who can find and report a bug.

Here's how it works in simple steps:

1. **The Company**: A company (like Google, Facebook, or a smaller business) wants to make sure their website, app, or software is secure and doesn't have any weaknesses that hackers could exploit.
2. **The Bug Hunter (You!)**: You, as a person interested in security (often called a "bug bounty hunter"), look for problems (bugs) in the company's software. These bugs might be things like flaws in the code, security holes, or other weaknesses that hackers could use to break into the system.
3. **Reporting the Bug**: If you find a bug, you report it to the company through their bug bounty program. You usually need to explain how you found the bug and how it could be used in a

harmful way.

4. **The Reward (Bounty)**: If the company agrees that your bug is serious and valuable, they will reward you with money or other prizes. The more severe the bug, the higher the reward can be. Some companies pay thousands of dollars for big bugs!

5. **Fixing the Bug**: After the company learns about the bug, they will work to fix it, making their software more secure for everyone

· **In simple terms: A bug bounty is a reward program where companies pay people to find and report bugs in their software to make it safer.**

· **How to become a bug bounty hunter :-**
· Get Familiar with Bug Bounty Platforms
· Before you start finding bugs, you need to know where companies run their bug bounty programs. Some of the most popular platforms are:-

1. HackerOne
2. Bugcrowd
3. Synack
4. Open Bug Bounty

- Sign up on one of these platforms. You'll need to create an account, and then you can start looking for websites or applications that are part of bug bounty programs.

Learn the Basics of Website Security

- To find bugs, it's helpful to know what types of bugs you're looking for. These are common categories of security bugs you might find:
- **Cross-Site Scripting (XSS)**: When a website allows someone to inject malicious code (like a virus) into a webpage. This could let hackers steal information or trick people into clicking on dangerous links.
- **SQL Injection**: When a website allows someone to inject harmful code into its database. This can let hackers steal or delete data.
- **Cross-Site Request Forgery (CSRF)**: When a malicious website tricks someone into performing actions they didn't intend on another website where they're logged in (like transferring money).
- **Broken Authentication**: When a website doesn't properly protect user login systems, which might allow attackers to log in as someone else.
- **Information Disclosure**: When a website accidentally shows sensitive information (like passwords or private data) to users or attackers

Tools You Can Use :-

- You don't need to be an expert to start finding bugs, but you will need some tools to help you check websites for weaknesses. Here are a few tools beginners can use:
- **Burp Suite (Free Version)**: A tool that helps you test websites for vulnerabilities. It can check for things like broken links, insecure pages, and other bugs.
- **OWASP ZAP**: Another free tool that helps you scan websites for security weaknesses.
- **Developer Tools in Your Browser**: Every web browser (like Chrome or Firefox) has built-in tools that can help you inspect the website's code, check for errors, or even look for things like login vulnerabilities.

Keep Learning and Improving

Finding bugs in websites takes practice. As you learn more about security and get better with tools like Burp Suite, you'll become more skilled at spotting issues. Keep reading, experimenting, and improving your skills!

- **Stay Ethical and Follow the Rules**

It's important to remember that bug bounty hunting is about helping companies make their websites safer. Always follow the rules of the bug bounty program. For example:

1. Don't test websites without permission (this is illegal).
2. Don't try to damage or steal data from websites.
3. Be respectful and professional when reporting bugs.

V
Dark Web

- **What is Dark Web?**
- The **dark web** is a part of the internet that isn't visible or accessible through regular search engines like Google. It exists on a special network called Tor, which stands for The **Onion Router**. To access the dark web, you need special software, like the Tor browser, which helps keep your identity and location hidden.

  While the regular internet is made up of websites you can easily find (like Facebook, Amazon, or Wikipedia), the dark web is much more private and secret. It is used by people who want to keep their online activities anonymous. Some of the content found there is perfectly legal and used for privacy reasons (like journalists or activists in repressive countries), but it's also known for illegal activities, such as black markets, hacking forums, and other things that are against the law.

- In simple terms, think of the regular web as the surface of an ocean, and the dark web is like the deep, hidden part beneath it, where only those with special tools can go.

- To access the dark web, you'll need to follow these steps carefully. It's important to understand that the dark web can host illegal activities, so you should be cautious and make sure you are following all laws and staying safe.

  Here's a simple step-by-step guide:
- **Step 1: Download and Install the Tor Browser**
- The Tor Browser is the main tool used to access the dark web. It allows you to browse websites anonymously.

1. Go to the official Tor website: https://www.torproject.or g/
2. Click on the "Download" button for your operating system (Windows, Mac, Linux).
3. Once downloaded, open the installer and follow the instructions to install the browser on your computer.

- **Step 2: Launch the Tor Browser**

1. Once it's installed:
2. Open the Tor Browser from your computer.
3. You will see a window asking you to either connect directly to the Tor network or configure your connection (usually, you can just click "Connect").
4. Wait for the connection to be established. This can take a minute or so.

- **Step 3: Browse the Dark Web**
- Now that you're connected to the Tor network, you can start browsing. Websites on the dark web end with .onion instead of .com or .org. These are special websites that can only be accessed through Tor.
- To find websites, you can search for dark web directories or lists of .onion sites (these can be found in search engines like DuckDuckGo).
- **For example**, you can try searching on a regular search engine for "dark web directories" or ".onion site lists," but be cautious

and make sure the links are legitimate.

- **Step 4: Stay Safe**
- **Avoid Illegal Activities**: There are many illegal and dangerous things on the dark web. Don't participate in anything illegal
- **Use a VPN**: Although Tor provides privacy, using a VPN (Virtual Private Network) can add an extra layer of security to keep your internet activity private.
- **Be Cautious:** Don't click on any suspicious links. Some websites on the dark web might contain malicious content like viruses or scams.
- **Step 5: Exit the Dark Web Safely**

Once you're done, you can simply close the Tor Browser. If you want to clear any traces of your browsing history:

- You can go into the Tor Browser settings and choose to clear your history or reset it.
- It's also good practice to restart your computer after using the dark web for extra privacy.

Additional Tips:

- **Don't share personal information**: Never share your real name, address, or any identifying details.
- **Use encrypted communication:** If you communicate with anyone, use secure messaging services like ProtonMail(for emails) or encrypted messaging platforms.
- **Be careful with financial transactions**: Some people use cryptocurrencies like Bitcoin on the dark web to protect their anonymity, but this also means there are risks involved. Be extra careful with your money.

"

That's the basic process! The key is to use Tor to access the dark web and be cautious at all times. If you stick to

legitimate uses (like privacy and security research), the dark web can be useful.
"

VI
Hacking Gadgets

Lets, learn about some Hacking gadgets,

    Flipper Zero :- Flipper Zero is a small, portable device designed for hardware hacking and cybersecurity experimentation. It's often used by ethical hackers, security researchers, and tech enthusiasts.

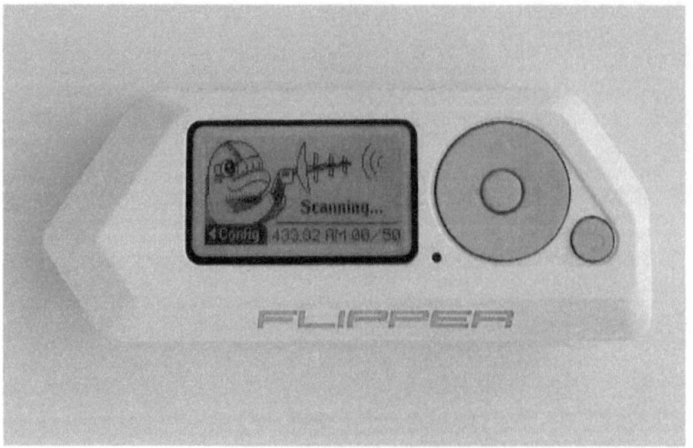

Flipper Zero

- **What Can Flipper Zero Do?**
- Flipper Zero can interact with a variety of wireless systems and electronic protocols. Here are some of the key things it can do:

1. RFID: It can read and emulate RFID cards (the kind used in office buildings or transit passes). So, if you have an RFID badge, Flipper Zero can copy the information and use it like the original card
2. Radio Signals (Sub-GHz): Flipper Zero can send and receive radio signals on a variety of frequencies. This means it can interact with garage door openers, car key fobs, wireless remotes, and other devices that use simple radio signals.
3. Infrared (IR): It can send infrared signals, just like a remote control. You can use it to control things like TVs, air conditioners, or other IRcontrolled devices.
4. -Wire and iButton: These are used in things like temperature sensors or key
     fobs for access control. Flipper Zero can read and emulate these devices.
5. GPIO Pins: Flipper Zero has
     General Purpose Input/Output (GPIO) pins, which allow you to connect it to other electronics for experimenting and hacking.

How Does Flipper Zero Work?

Flipper Zero works by sending signals (radio, infrared, etc.) or reading data from various types of electronic systems. It has built-in antennas and sensors that allow it to communicate with different devices. The main thing that makes Flipper Zero useful is that it can both read and emulate or send these signals. This means it can copy information from one device and use it with another, or test the security of a system.

For example:

1. If you want to test the security of a garage door opener, Flipper Zero can read the signal that the remote sends when you press a button. Then, it can replay that signal to open the door.
2. If you're working with an RFID system, Flipper Zero can scan the RFID tag to grab its information, and then later "pretend" to be that RFID tag by sending the same signal

"For More information you can checkout video tutorial on youtube How Flipper Zero works"

What is Bad Usb :- Normally, a USB device (like a keyboard or flash drive) only does what it's supposed to do. For example, a keyboardsends keystrokes when you press the keys, and a flash drive stores files. However, BadUSB takes advantage of a weakness in the way USB devices are designed. It can trick your computer into thinking a regular device (like a USB flash drive) is actually a keyboard or mouse, which can then send commands to your computer—like opening websites, running programs, or even installing viruses.

- **How Does BadUSB Work?**
- A BadUSB device looks like a normal USB device, but it is specially programmed to act differently. **For example:**

If you plug in a flash drive that has been turned into a BadUSB device, your computer might think it's a keyboardinstead. As a keyboard, it could secretly type commands into your computer, like opening a terminal or running harmful scripts. This could give a hacker control over your computer without you ever knowing.

Bad Usb

Real-World Example:
Imagine you plug in a USB stick (that has been modified into a BadUSB device) into your computer. You think it's just a normal flash drive, but in reality, it starts sending commands to the computer like this:

- It opens a command prompt (a place where a computer can execute instructions).
- It types in malicious commands to download a virus or install spyware.
- It runs these commands before you even realize what's happening.

Why is it Dangerous?
BadUSB is dangerous because it can work invisibly. You don't need to click on anything or run a suspicious file. Just plugging in the USB device is enough to allow the attacker to control the

computer and execute harmful actions.

- It can be used to:

1. Steal sensitive information (like passwords).
2. Install viruses or malware
3. Disable antivirus software

- **Is BadUSB Legal?**
- Using BadUSB for malicious purposes (like hacking someone's computer without permission) is illegal. However, using it for ethical hacking (such as testing the security of your own devices or for research purposes) may be allowed, depending on the laws in your country

Can You Protect Yourself?

Yes, there are ways to protect your computer from BadUSB attacks:

Be cautious with USB devices: Only plug in USB devices from trusted sources. Avoid using random USB sticks found in public places, like USB drives left behind in public areas.

1. **Use USB port locks**: On some computers, you can disable USB ports or use USB security software that blocks unauthorized devices.
2. **Keep Your system updated**
3. **Use a hardware firewall**: Some hardware devices can monitor USB ports and block suspicious activity.

What is OMG Cable :-

- An **OMG Cable** is a type of hacking tool that looks like a normal charging cable (such as a USB cable), but it's actually a sneaky device that can be used to hijack or control a computer or phone when plugged in. It's part of a group of tools used in "USB attacks" to exploit devices without the owner realizing what's happening.

In short, omg cable is :-
The OMG Cable looks just like a regular USB charging cable, but it has been modified with special hardware inside. When you plug it into a computer or phone, it can secretly do things like:

1. Steal data (like passwords, files, or information).
2. Control the device (open programs, access the internet, etc.
3. Send commands to the device (just like a keyboard or mouse would).

- **How Does OMG Cable Work?**
- The OMG Cable works in a similar way to the BadUSB attack, but it has some advanced features:

1. **Simulates keyboard input:** It can make the computer or phone think the cable is a keyboard, and then it can type in commands, open applications, or run malicious programs automatically.
2. **Wireless control**: Some OMG Cables are designed to be wireless. They can connect to a nearby attacker's device (like a phone or laptop) and let the attacker control the target device remotely, without the target person knowing.

How Does Someone Use an OMG Cable?
Here's how someone might use an OMG Cable:

- The attacker places the OMG Cable somewhere the victim will plug it in— like in a coffee shop or airport, or even inside a device they own (for example, swapping out a regular USB cable with the OMG Cable).
- Once plugged into the victim's computer or phone, the OMG Cable can do things like:

- Steal sensitive data (such as passwords or credit card information). , Give remote access to an attacker without the victim knowing.

Why Is It Dangerous?

The OMG Cable is dangerous because it works **silently** and **automatically.** The person who plugs it into their device won't see anything unusual happening. In fact, it might seem like a regular charging cable, but in reality, it's performing actions in the background. This makes it difficult to detect because it doesn't require any clicks or interactions from the victim—everything happens just by plugging in the cable.

- **In Summary:** An OMG Cable is a hacker tool that looks like a regular USB charging cable, but it can secretly control or hack a computer or phone when plugged in. It can send commands, steal data, or even give someone remote access to your device. To stay safe, don't plug in unknown cables, use data-blocking devices, and always be cautious with USB connection

Is OMG Cable Legal?

Using an OMG Cable for ethical hacking (such as testing the security of your own devices or for research purposes) can be legal. However, using it to hack into someone else's device without permission is illegal and unethical. Always make sure you're using such tools responsibly and within the law.

- **How Can You Protect Yourself from OMG Cable Attacks?**

To stay safe from attacks using OMG Cables (or similar tools), here are some tips:

1. **Don't plug in unknown USB cables:** Be careful about using USB cables you find in public places or get from strangers. Only use cables from trusted sources

2. **Use a USB data blocker**: A USB data blocker is a device that only allows charging, but it blocks any data transfer between the cable and your device.

3. **Disable USB ports**: Some people disable USB ports on their devices when not needed, especially in highsecurity environments.

4. **Check for unusual behavior**: If your computer or phone starts acting strangely after plugging in a cable (like opening programs, typing by itself, or showing new files), it might be a sign of an attack.

What is Wifi- Pineapple :- Wi-Fi Pineapple looks like a regular Wi-Fi router, but it's much more powerful and has special features for security testing. It's made by a company called Hak5, and it's designed to be used for testing the security of Wi-Fi networks, helping find weaknesses, and discovering vulnerabilities.

Wifi Pineapple

How Does It Work?

To make it simple, imagine you're at a coffee shop and there are several Wi-Fi networks around you. Here's how the Wi-Fi Pineapple might work:

- **Step 1:** The Wi-Fi Pineapple creates its own fake Wi-Fi network that looks just like the coffee shop's network (but with a different name or identical name).
- **Step 2**: People nearby who are looking for Wi-Fi might connect to the fake network thinking it's the legitimate one. Once they're connected, the Wi-Fi Pineapple can observe everything they do, like websites they visit or login credentials they enter.
- **Step 3**: The Wi-Fi Pineapple can also modify the data being sent or even redirect the user to malicious websites without them realizing it. It can capture passwords, personal information, and other sensitive data being transmitted over the WiFi connection.

VII

How To Work with Government as an ethical hacker

Working with the government as an ethical hacker can be a highly rewarding and impactful career path. Governments often rely on ethical hackers (or "white- hat" hackers) to strengthen their cybersecurity defenses, identify vulnerabilities, and protect sensitive data from malicious attacks. Here are some steps and strategies for working with government entities as an ethical hacker:

- **Learn the Basics of Ethical Hacking**

What is Ethical Hacking?
Ethical hackers, or "white-hat" hackers, are people who find and fix security problems in computer systems to prevent cybercriminals from exploiting them.

Start with the basics: Learn how computers, networks, and the internet work. Familiarize yourself with key concepts like network security, firewalls, and encryption.

- **Get Some Certifications**
- Governments look for certified experts. You can start with certifications that show you know how to ethically hack and protect systems:

Certified Ethical Hacker (CEH): This is a popular certification that teaches you the skills to find weaknesses in a system, just like a hacker would, but in a legal and ethical way.

- **CompTIA Security+**: A good starting point for learning basic cybersecurity concepts.

Understand the Rules

Stay Legal: As an ethical hacker, you must always work within the law. Never hack into systems without permission. The government will only want to work with you if you're following the rules.

- **Confidentiality**: When you find security issues in government systems, you have to report them responsibly and keep them private. This means not sharing any sensitive information you discover.
-

Work with the Government

- Look for government job openings: Many governments have cybersecurity teams that hire ethical hackers. You can apply for these jobs if you have the right certifications and experience.
- **Cybersecurity Companies**: Some private companies work with the government to help secure systems. You could join one of these companies and work on government projects as a contractor.
- **Participate in government-led programs**: Some governments offer programs where ethical hackers can help identify security

flaws in their systems.These programs are often advertised online.

·

·

"Keep Learning and Stay Updated"

- Cybersecurity is always changing. To stay useful to the government, you need to keep learning and practicing your skills.
- **Follow cybersecurity news:** Stay up to date on the latest hacking techniques, threats, and security trends.

- Continue practicing: Keep using platforms like Hack The Box or CTF challenges to improve your skills.

In Simple Steps:

1. Learn the basics of computers and networks.
2. Get certified in ethical hacking (like CEH or Security+).
3. Practice hacking in safe environments and try bug bounty programs.
4. Stay within the law and act responsibly.
5. Look for government job openings or programs where you can use your skills.
6. Keep learning and improving your skills.

By following these steps, you'll be able to contribute to the government's cybersecurity efforts and help protect important systems and data.

- agencies like the **Intelligence Bureau (IB)** and the **Central Bureau of Investigation (CBI)** in India do hire cybersecurity professionals, including ethical hackers. These agencies, along with other government security and intelligence agencies, play a crucial role in national security, law enforcement, and preventing cybercrime, which requires skilled cybersecurity experts to protect critical information and systems.

Other Government Agencies That Hire Ethical Hackers:
Besides the IB and CBI, several other Indian government agencies and ministries also hire ethical hackers, including:

- National Technical Research Organisation (NTRO): A technical intelligence agency involved in cyber security and cyber intelligence.
- National Investigation Agency (NIA): Investigates national security-related crimes, including cyberterrorism
- Defense Research and Development Organisation (DRDO): Works on military cybersecurity and defense technologies.
- Ministry of Electronics and Information Technology(MeitY): Has initiatives like the Indian Computer EmergencyResponse Team (CERT- In) that hires cybersecurity experts.
- Indian Army & Air Force: Have their own cybersecurity divisions and hire ethical hackers for defense-related roles.

VIII
What is Cyberbullying

Cyberbullying :- Cyberbullying is when someone uses the internet, social media, or other digital platforms to hurt, threaten, or embarrass another person. It's like bullying, but it happens online instead of in person.

- **Key Points to Understand Cyberbullying**:
- Using Technology to Hurt Others: Cyberbullying happens through things like:

1. Social media (Facebook, Instagram,Twitter)
2. Text messages or emails
3. Online games or forums
4. Websites or blogs

It Can Be Done Anonymously: Sometimes, the person bullying can hide behind a fake name or profile, which makes it harder for others to know who is responsible.

- **Forms of Cyberbullying:**

1. **Harassment**: Repeatedly sending hurtful messages or comments.

2. **Spreading Lies**: Sharing false information or rumors to damage someone's reputation
3. **Exclusion**: Intentionally leaving someone out of a group chat or social event online
4. **Impersonation:** Pretending to be someone else online and saying harmful things in their name.
5. **Outing:** Sharing private information, photos, or videos without permission to embarrass someone.

Effects of Cyberbullying:

1. The person being bullied may feel sad, anxious, or even scared
2. It can affect their self-esteem and make them feel isolated.
3. In some severe cases, it can lead to serious mental health problems or harm.

What to Do About Cyberbullying:

- **Report it**: Most social media platforms or websites have options to report bullying behavior.
- **Block the Bully:** Blocking the person who is bullying you can stop them from contacting you.
- **Talk to Someone:** It's important to talk to a trusted adult (parent, teacher, or cyber expert if you're being bullied online.

Simple Example:

- Imagine you're a student, and someone at your school keeps posting mean things about you on Instagram or sending nasty messages. This is a form of cyberbullying. Even though they're not physically near you, their words can still hurt and affect you emotionally.

In Summary:

- Cyberbullying is using digital tools like the internet or social media to hurt or embarrass others. It's a serious issue that can harm people's mental health, but there are ways to handle it, like reporting, blocking, and getting support from trusted people.

-

- In India, cyberbullying is a form of online harassment and can be addressed through various provisions under the Indian Penal Code (IPC), Information Technology Act (IT Act), and other related laws.

Section 354D of the IPC – Stalking: Cyberstalking is a form of online harassment where the bully repeatedly monitors or follows someone's online presence, sending unwelcome messages or threats. This section of the IPC makes stalking (including cyberstalking) a punishable offense.

- **Section 499 of the IPC – Defamation**: If a person spreads false or malicious information online that harms your reputation, this can be considered defamation.

Section 499 defines defamation as when someone makes or publishes false statements that damage the reputation of a person. If the defamation is done through digital platforms, such as social media, it is still covered under Section 499.

- **Steps to File a Complaint for Cyberbullying**:

1. Gather Evidence: Screenshots: Take clear screenshots of the abusive messages, posts, comments, or content.
2. Record Details: If possible, note the date, time, and any other information (like the name or profile details) of the person bullying you. '
3. Save Digital Evidence: Keep a record of the messages or emails in their original form, without editing or deleting anything.

File a Complaint with the Police:

1. You can visit the Cyber Crime Cell of your local police station, or file a complaint online if your state provides an online reporting system
2. Provide all the evidence you've gathered, and explain how you've been cyberbullied.
3. If the police station does not have a dedicated Cyber Crime Cell, they are still obligated to help you report cybercrimes under the IT Act and the IPC.

File a Complaint with the National Cyber Crime Reporting Portal:

- The Indian government has a National Cyber Crime Reporting Portal (cybercrime.gov.in) where you can register a complaint related to cybercrimes, including cyberbullying, online harassment, or cyberstalking. This portal helps in reporting crimes related to technology across India.

File a Defamation Lawsuit:

- If your reputation is damaged by false information or malicious content shared online, you can file a defamation lawsuit under Section 499 of the IPC.

Contact Online Platforms:

1. Most social media platforms, websites, and messaging apps allow you to report cyberbullying or abusive content directly through their own reporting systems
2. After reporting, the platform may take down the offensive content, block the bully, or suspend their account.

IX

How To File a Complaint against CyberFraud

"The National Cyber Crime Helpline number in India is:"

1930

You can call 1930 to report any cybercrime, including cyber fraud, cyberbullying, online harassment, hacking, identity theft, and more. The helpline is available to assist victims and guide them through the process of reporting cybercrimes.

- Additionally, you can visit the National Cyber Crime Reporting Portal for filing complaints online: **cybercrime.gov.in**

Key Points:

- Helpline Number: 1930 (for reporting cybercrimes).
- Website: https://cybercrime.gov.in/ (for filing online complaints).

Steps to File a Complaint for Cyber Fraud in India:

- File a Complaint with the Police

1. You can go to your local police station to file a First Information Report (FIR). If the police station has a Cyber Crime Cell, you can directly approach them, as they handle cyber fraud cases.
2. Many police stations in India have a dedicated Cyber Crime Cell to specifically handle cases of online fraud and cybercrimes.

File a Complaint on the National Cyber Crime Reporting Portal :-

The National Cyber Crime Reporting Portal (cybercrime.gov.in) is the official platform launched by the Indian government to report. cybercrimes, including cyber fraud. This platform allows individuals to register complaints online from anywhere in India.

- **Steps to file on the portal:**

1. Visit the official portal: Cyber Crime Reporting Portal
2. Select the appropriate category (e.g.,Cyber Fraud, Online Fraud).
3. Fill in the details of the incident (description of the fraud, personal information, etc.).
4. Upload any supporting evidence (like screenshots of fraudulent transactions or communications).
5. Submit the complaint, and you'll receive a reference number for tracking your case.

X

About The Author

yash hackz

In the beginning, it wasn't easy. I faced many challenges. Lets, i share my journey how i became an ethical Hacker -

- My journey into the world of Ethical Hacking began during a difficult time in my life, marked by hardship and loss. When I was in 1st grade, I lost my father to a *heart attack*. Since then, my mother has been my greatest support, helping me get to where I am today."

yash hackz' Father

So, my story starts here. I was in 9th grade at that time And I was quite an introvert, I didn't even have friends in school. and I didn't have a personal phone. And obviously, I couldn't even ask my family for one, because I knew our financial condition wasn't good at that time. At that time, I had a useless keypad phone at my home, and I started using it. Opera Mini browser was already installed on that phone, and I created a Facebook account using that keypad phone. After that, I met a girl on Facebook, and we became friends. after that Slowly, we started talking, and both of us began sharing our thoughts. Then, one day, we had a fight over something, and she ended up blocking me. Now, I was getting worried. I had to get unblocked, so... After school every day, I decided to take my brother's phone by telling him that I needed to clear some study doubts. But instead of studying, I started watching hacking tutorials on YouTube. Like how to unblock itself on facebook. I began doing this every day. Then, one day, I tried a method, and **I got unblocked.**

"After that, I became interested in hacking."

Then, one day, I asked my brother to buy me a personal phone, but he refused directly. Then, I focused completely on my studies. When I graduated from 9th grade, I received the award for 100% attendance. After that, my brother was happy and gifted me my first Android phone. That day was the best day of my life. Then, I continued learning hacking by searching online tutorials, reading blogs, and exploring Wikipedia. overall i learned hacking self. After some time, I gained experience, and then I decided that I would help people with hacking. So, I posted on Facebook, asking if anyone needed help related to hacking?

"Then,"

There, I received messages from some people, and I started helping them. Overall, I began doing paid work for people, My First earning was 1k inr that i got after helping a client to recover his fb account.

Then everyone at home came to know that I do hacking. After That, I found a client on Facebook, completed the work for him, i secured his website, then that client asked me questions like what's my age n all He said he wants to meet me and unfortunately i can't believe the client gave me a laptop as a gift after met. And it was the first step of my life changing. Then, my relatives also came to know that I was into hacking, and they told my mother in a harsh manner that He would do wrong things in the future using hacking. *My mom felt bad that day she cried from that day I decided that one day, I would prove to everyone that hackers are not always wrong.* Then, from that laptop, I started learning advanced level hacking and programming languages.

"*Year 2022,*"

After some time, when I gained experience, I applied for several exams, such as CEH , OSCP

And yes, I successfully passed exams like CEH and other similar certifications. After that, I focused more on my learning and then

continued to improve my skills.

"9ᵗʰ April 2022,"

I had collected data from some fraud apps, including loan apps, which were gathering personal information of Indian people, such as details from their Aadhar Card and PAN Card. and they were misusing them. So, I provided the data and information about those fraudulent apps to the government. So, I received a reward of $1500 from the government. That day, my News, was published, and it was a proud moment for me.

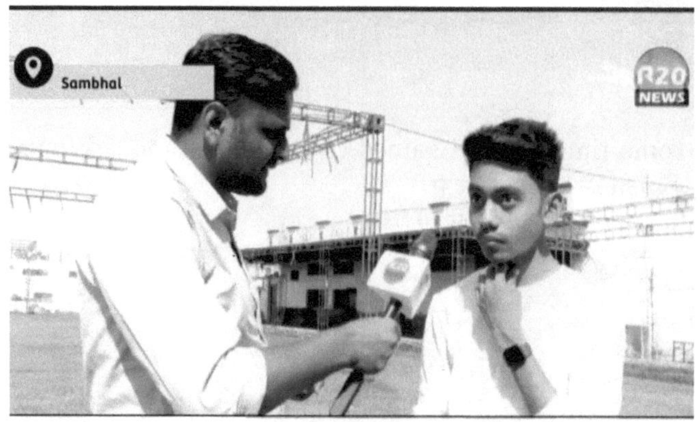

yash hackz'

Then, After 2 months, I started working as a cybersecurity analyst in a company. And also I created a YouTube channel and decided to make cybersecurity knowledge based videos. And yes.. I gained 18,000 subscribers on my channel in just 3 months. I was very happy at that time, so I decided to gift a car to my family with my first earning.

yash hackz'

I had also fulfilled this dream, and my Family felt very proud that day.

yash hackz' Mother

Everything was going well in my life, but one day, my friends did multiple bot reports on my channel, and it was removed from YouTube. That day, I felt lost and cried, but my mother supported me. She said, 'We are with you. Start again, and everything will be fine. But I had lost my faith and felt that nothing would get better now. My family members encouraged me to create a new channel and start again

- After 3 months, I created a new YouTube channel, and in just 5 months, I reached 100k subscribers on that channel.

From this, I learned that whatever happens, happens for the best.

yash hackz' Silver Play button

"The story continues............"

yash hackz' Family

"One thing i would like to say, You will Never Change your Life until you change the habits you do daily. The Secret of your Success is Found in your daily routine"

-Crying does not indicate that you are weak. Since birth it has always been a sign that you are alive

- "Yeh thi meri kahani! baaki, Agar kuch achha laga ho, toh zaroor batana. Mujhe yeh samajh aaya ke life mein kabhi bhi sab kuch asaan nahi hota, Saayad kuch log mere life mein mujhe giraane na aate toh main kabhi success nahi kar pata. Unhone jo kuch bhi kaha, jo kuch bhi kiya, usne mujhe apni asli taqat dikhayi. Unhi logon ke wajah se maine seekha ke jab tak tum gir nahi jaoge, tab tak tumhe uthna aur aage badhna ka asli maza nahi pata chalega. I still remember ek baar bachpan mein maine kisi ko bola tha, ki one day i will buy my own car Saayad uss time ye immaturity thi but jab ego hurt hota hai toh we can do anything possible. Toh agar aap bhi struggle kar rahe ho, ya koi aapko neecha dikhane ki koshish kar raha hai, toh bas yeh yaad rakho: unki baaton ko apni taqat banao, aur apni life , career ko apne tareeqe se Jiyo......."

"If You Really wanna grow in Life. Toh Tumhe bhaout Saari Cheezo ko Peeche chodhna padega Ho skta hai tumhe apna sheher Apni purani memories, Apne dost Aur specially apna comfort Zone Sab chodhna pade kyunki life mein kuch bhi bina gawaye ya bina sacrifice kare kabhi nhi milta Aur yaad rakhna. Even heaven demands death in return."